Cover design by Dee Anderson

Printed by Sentinel Printing, St. Cloud, Minnesota
http://www.sentinelprinting.com

Third printing 2015

IQ OF 63 SO WHAT?

GOING BEYOND EVERYBODY ELSE'S EXPECTATIONS

BY

BEN D. ANDERSON

with foreword written by
Ashleigh Molloy, PhD

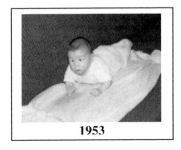

1953

Crippled Children's School

Benny & his Grandpa

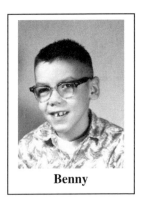

Benny

1974

1978

I dedicate this book to my parents,
Russell and Marlys Anderson, who taught me to
"Go for it!"
I love them very much

Acknowledgements

Thank you to all my friends who were my readers

Thank you to Dr. Ashleigh Molloy, PhD,
Director, Transformation Education Institute, Toronto
Professor, York University, Toronto, Canada
who wrote the foreword

Thank you to the Rev. Dick Beckmen
who helped me in editing the book
and for his friendship and support.

Thank you to Pinckney Hall, PhD for all his help.

Thank you to my lovely wife Dee
who stands by me and who typed the book,,
Thank you Honey!

Foreword

"This book is deeply touching as Ben shares his journey through life. Ben's story takes us from disappointments to his goal focused pursuit as a person filled with gifts to share with others. His story telling begins with his birth on the prairies of North Dakota. We are shown the strength and deep devotion of his parents and family as they sought the necessary support services. The special bond with his grandfather demonstrates the precious gift of a loving relationship. Ben's recollections validate for us the need to feel bonded with others and recognize the importance of family. His stories are filled with tenderness and introspection. He expresses his dreams and the challenges he faced. Ben ardently pursues these dreams and will not be swayed from reaching his goals.

His romantic journey is shared and reflects both humorous and sensitive moments. Ben with his wife and soul mate Dee currently travel around the nation bringing precious hope through his presentations. He offers his audiences encouragement and inspiration to be the best they can be.

Testing scores relegated Ben to the bottom of the group yet Ben defied the results. He proved that perseverance coupled with loving support from family and friends are enablers of results that can only be described as "supercalifragilisticexpialidocious".

Ben welcomes us joyously into his life experiences and proves categorically that he has surpassed the expectations of his 63 IQ. As pilgrims traveling on the road of life Ben provides us with a destination and a purpose. I am proud to have such a wonderful friend and it is definitely an honor and privilege for me to have been asked to provide the foreword."

Dr. Ashleigh Molloy
Director
Transformation Education Institute

Reviews

"As a mother of a child "labeled" as having a disability, I feel Ben Anderson's "*IQ of 63- So what!*' is a must reading for parents and professionals of individuals with disabilities. Rarely are the experiences of having a disability and its impact on one's life so simply yet eloquently retold as through the direct, honest voice of Ben Anderson. You will find yourself cheering for Ben through every page as he expertly leads the reader through the up's and down's of the life of a person born with cerebral palsy in the 1950's. If you or someone you love has ever been told to "give up" or "be realistic" about their dreams: you need to read this book."
Sandra Padmanabhan, Ph.D.

"Ben's story gives us more than a message to think about, it provides a tool for us to teach and learn from. "
Donna Halverson, 5th grade teacher"

"Ben Anderson is a remarkable man. He has established lofty goals for himself and has achieved them. Ben's relationships with his friends and his presentations to thousands of persons over the years have brought positive turnabouts in how we view and interact with individuals with disabilities. Ben's book is a mirror into his life from infancy to this day. We meet the persons who saw the true Ben, and those who placed upon him the lowest of expectations. We encounter Ben's hopes, faith and persistence. Those attributes provide a lesson for ours. This book deserves a wide audience and discussion over many cups of coffee!"

(Rev) Harvey Stower, Mayor, Amery, WI

"An easy but profound read which is important as it can be shared with people of all intellectual levels. It really touches home for those who are raising children with disabilities as it allows for the perspective that children would love to share but many times can't for a variety of reasons. The quintessential story of the value vs. detriment of labels. Yes, they can help drive services, but they can also create boxes that are hard to break out of. Thanks for your continuing work on behalf of those who live daily with the reality, difficulty and joys of disability."- *Jennifer Newhouse, Parent to Parent Coordinator, Washington State.*

"This book is a "must read" for all folks that will be interacting with people with disabilities – which should be ALL of us. Ben's very thoughtful look at himself and realization that things should and could have been different if he were born later in the century, is a sensitive way to deal with the issue of neglect and discrimination in our educational system and society. Ben is a survivor!! Miraculously, his determination and will were not stifled and he is able to "make a difference" in the lives of those he comes into contact with. He has spoken to thousands of students in the classes in teacher preparation at UW-Stout. His message is clear as he shares "his story" and then explains to the students why Inclusion in the classroom is so important for students with disabilities. He is an inspiration and a strong advocate for those with disabilities and their parents and the teachers that willingly teach them."

Lynn LaVenture, Instructor, UW-Stout

UW-Stout-1992

Advocacy

Wedding day!

After the conferences & workshops

Open forum talk

INDEX

xiii

Chapter One
"Happiness is a new child"

The time was late fall. The trees were quickly losing their leaves. You could sense in the air that winter would soon be upon us. The year was 1952.

She went to the doctor and got the news that she was pregnant. At this point in her life the thought of being pregnant was a very good thought. This would be her second child. News travels fast in a small town and soon most people knew that she was expecting a child. In fact, there were other women expecting in her church circle as well.

Their first child Terri was about two years old. When she heard the news she became very excited. She was going to have a new sister or brother to play with instead of just fantasizing about a playmate. One day her parents heard her explaining this to her dolls, "Do you know that Mommy is going to have a baby." Hearing their daughter that excited only made the parents happier to receive this new child.

1

This was a wonderful time for this couple. Marlys and Russell were caught up in great anticipation. They wondered what sort of boy or girl they would have. Their friends were excited as well and embraced their joy. But first, they had to go through the winter on the prairies of North Dakota. It was cold and the parents had to work hard since they did not have a lot of resources. But this in no way diminished their excitement within and the overflowing joy in their words and faces.

"Mommy, is it going to happen soon? I want to play with the baby." "No, it is not time, but not very long. The baby will come in the summer."

That spring was a busy time for the parents as they prepared themselves and their home for a second child.

It was Tuesday, June 16, 1953 at 1:10 in the morning when it happened. Marlys and Russell had a new son. Their excitement was unbelievable. Terri, the two and a half year old sister, didn't need to fantasize any longer. She took her dolls to see the baby and proudly exclaimed, "This is my new brother!" Marlys and Russell named the boy Benny Dean. He was named after his grandfather Bennie. Benny would come to have a great relationship with his grandfather.

As time went on his parents noticed that Benny wasn't making normal progress; he hadn't begun to walk or talk. They took him to the family doctor and the news of his diagnosis was a shock. Benny had cerebral palsy. Russell and Marlys were not even sure what that meant. Marlys did not know what feelings to feel. She was unable to comprehend what exactly it might mean for them all. "Why me?" ran through her head. "What can I do and will I be able to care for him?" She was filled with conflicting emotions. It was her child they were talking about in that office. There were so many questions and no answers. She was at the beginning of a long journey to discover what the words, "cerebral palsy" meant. She grabbed every book she could that would help explain his condition. Their attention now needed to shift to begin a plan for Benny's medical situation.

The grandfather Bennie played a strong role in loving and challenging his namesake. This was especially true with regard to Benny's inability to walk. One day the boy and his grandfather went to the John Deere shop to pick up some parts. Benny could not walk so he sat on the floor and played while his grandfather was doing business. He spied a small John Deere pedal tractor. As his grandfather turned and looked at him, he saw that Benny was enchanted by the tractor. He had climbed up on it and was sitting in the seat. He knew his grandson wanted this tractor but could not have it that day. Grandpa said to Benny, *"If you can learn to walk I promise to buy you that John Deere pedal tractor."* That was Benny's first real challenge.

As Marlys and Russell began to research the next step for Benny's education and therapy, they realized that it was not going to be easy. There was nothing in their home area for someone with Benny's medical needs.

Their family doctor recommended that they go and check out the Crippled Children's School in Jamestown. It was a long way from their home but they had to keep their son's welfare in mind.

The summer of 1957 had to have been a roller coaster of emotions for the parents. They were told that the best place for Benny was the Crippled Children's School in Jamestown, North Dakota which they had previously investigated. This meant Benny would be 250 miles away from home. It was a difficult decision since there was no job available for Russell in Jamestown and it made visiting Benny difficult because of the distance. The emotional struggle was clear. Here is a boy at the age of three and a half being told he needed to go to another place far from home and parents.

In July of that year Benny was taken to get a re-evaluation at the Crippled Children's School. The two weeks of testing were certainly one of the hardest times for Marlys and Russell. They watched as their son was run through all kinds of tests. They wanted to know but it was painful as they began to hear the results. It was a very difficult moment when this father and mother were told that their son had a very low IQ. The evaluation showed an IQ in the low 60's. He was declared mildly retarded. They thought there could be no way this was true. It was another major setback for their son. They could not imagine what the future was to be like for him. The school recommended that he come back in the fall and begin classes. Benny had many needs that the school could meet. It was a place where Benny could get a comprehensive education and the therapy he needed to be on the right track. Even though it was difficult for them to hear this they knew they needed to look at their son's needs. This seemed to be the only answer and it was a good answer, even though painful because of the separation.

The re-evaluation was finished in late July and his parents brought Benny back home for a month before he had to go back to start school. Then he would be separated from his parents and sister. But wait! Don't forget the tractor! Grandpa Bennie brought the tractor over one day before Benny was to leave. Benny had learned to walk and his grandfather knew how badly Benny wanted that green tractor. When Benny saw the tractor he was excited. He enjoyed country life on the farm, especially the machinery. The tractor went with him to Jamestown and was a constant reminder of home. At the school he was able to peddle his tractor. He pretended he was a farmer like his father and grandfather. He drove his green John Deere up and down the hallways. It is said that you can take the boy out of the country but you cannot take the country out of the boy. That statement was true for Benny. He loved the country and all that went with it. That tractor was a saving grace. It kept him in touch with all that he had left at home.

When September came the most difficult part of the arrangement happened. Benny lay down in the grass as his parents drove away and he cried as he watched the car disappear over the hill, heading northwest. Benny's father often mentioned that the ride home that day seemed pretty long. There was not much talking between husband and wife as they left their boy with a bunch of strangers. If one of them had said, "let's go back," they would have. They knew it was the best thing for their son.

Vacations from the school were few and far between and phone calls were only allowed every other week after a six weeks waiting period. The weekly letters that Marlys wrote to her son seemed to satisfy a young mother's desire to be with her child. Her letters were a connection that tried to maintain a sense of closeness. The six weeks of waiting to communicate were especially difficult. "Maybe we should take the long trip to visit Benny and stay at a hotel." his mother suggested.

Chapter Two
"The Emotions of Letting Go"

"I miss my mommy and daddy really badly." "I wish my mommy and daddy would come to see me and I really do miss my sister."

We used to have so much fun playing together. I have kids I play with now in Jamestown, but they are new and I don't know where they come from. The kids are nice to me. But, I miss my mommy and daddy when I go to bed at night. *"Where is Mommy?"* I need her to tuck me in and say my prayers. I am lonely. I cry every night. I wish mommy and daddy were here.

"Look Benny, you have a letter from mommy and daddy!"

Dear Benny,
We miss you so much. Guess what? Daddy and Terri and I are coming to see you and bring you a pumpkin for Halloween. We will stay for a week and maybe

you can stay in the hotel with us. We will get up early on Saturday morning and will be there by 10:00 am.

Love, Mommy, Daddy and Terri

Mealtime was always an important time for us, but even more important was the class time when the teacher would read the letters from home. I was so excited to hear that my family was coming. It seemed like a long time since they were here. Hearing the news made that day the most wonderful day of my life. I could not get my mind off the weekend. But I still had work to do.

I had speech therapy to go to. I liked speech class. The teacher gave me peanut butter when I did well. I loved peanut butter. The teacher was nice to me and tried hard to help me sound out my words. I had a very small vocabulary. My first word was moo. Moo this and moo that. It was the only word I used. The word was important to me since I came from a farm. The word moo was the way cows communicated. Everything in my universe was moo. I liked my teacher. She worked hard to get me to speak. The peanut butter helped too. *Maybe someday I will be able to tell Mommy, Daddy and Terri that I love them.* Speech therapy was a very important part of my weekly activities.

There were many other classes that I had too. I learned my ABC's. Physical therapy was important as well since I had difficulty walking. After class I would ride my tractor up and down the halls. My friends joined me on their tricycles. We would pretend we were racing. I had a wagon my dad built attached to the back of my tractor. Sometimes I hauled my friends in the wagon; they liked to ride in it.

After playtime we went to the big dining room. It was a huge room with many windows. I missed sitting at the table with my family. I reached in my pocket and took out the letter from my folks. I asked someone to read it again. I was so eager to see them and stay with them in the hotel. All I could keep saying was moo, moo, moo.

After supper we went to our bedroom. It was not like my bedroom at home. This was another big room. There were beds in rows along the wall. A lot of kids slept in this room, maybe eight or nine. No one tucked me into bed. There was no mommy or daddy to say goodnight to me. As I put the letter on the nightstand next to my bed I was reminded of home and the farm. I couldn't wait until tomorrow morning. Mommy and daddy would be here. They said they would be here at ten. I would watch to see if I can see their car coming down the hill. But, in the morning I found out it was only Friday! I had to wait one more day.

Friday was the day I worked on physical therapy. They showed me how to dress and undress myself. I liked doing that and I tried to do it faster and faster. I imagined I was a fireman and I wanted to learn how to dress quickly and slide down the pole to get to a fire. Physical therapy helped me a lot.

Today is Saturday!!

"Mommy and Daddy, how are you? I love you (moo, moo, moo, moo)." I hugged them and hugged them and kissed them. Terri said, "Look what we brought you." It was a pumpkin. Halloween was coming soon and Daddy and I carved out the pumpkin. It was so good to be with them. Dad had carved a real funny face on the pumpkin and when they put it on my nightstand I laughed and laughed. Mom said, "Let's go out to eat at a restaurant." I wanted to ride in the car and get to the hotel so badly. *I am so happy. We will be alone as a family.* I could hardly believe it was really happening.

We spent that night in a hotel. It was so much fun. We played fun games and laughed some more about the pumpkin.

They told me that they had to leave in the morning for home. *"Why did they have to leave? Can I go home with them?"* I want to go home. I want to see grandma and grandpa. Daddy told me that I would be able to go home at Christmas for two weeks. Christmas was just a few weeks away. It seemed like it was going to be forever to me. *Bye, Mommy. Bye, Daddy. Bye, Terri. Moo. Moo. Moo. Moo.*

It was back to my routine. I rode my tractor. I played with Teddy, my friend. I remembered the good time I had over the weekend. Moo. Therapy…peanut butter I like it. . . . "Did you have a good time, Benny?" "Yeah!" "Try to say mommy and daddy, you can do it." "Move that tongue." "Isn't that peanut butter good?"

"Look, Benny. You have another letter and a box of cookies from your grandma." The letter read,
> *"We will see you at Christmas time.*
> *Santa Claus will be here."*

I can hardly wait! Grandpa, grandma and Santa Claus all at the same time!

"Benny, you have a phone call." Mommy and Daddy were on the line. They reminded me that I would soon be home for Christmas. They told me someone else was waiting for me at home. "We bought you a dog.

His name is Shep." Good things were happening for me. I couldn't wait to play with my new dog.

Christmas Eve was cold and crisp. There was snow on the ground. The snow sparkled as we made our way to grandma's house. We ate oyster soup with those small crackers that looked like stars. A knock on the door interrupted us. When the door was opened Santa Claus came into the room. What a funny looking guy. He brought many presents. My sister and I wanted to play all night.

Christmas Day was also spent at Grandpa and Grandma's house. Many other relatives came and celebrated. Grandpa wanted to know how I liked my John Deere tractor. I said, "Moo." This meant I loved it. My vocabulary was still not very developed. I had made some progress. There were new words that I had learned. Everybody was happy to see my progress with speech.

I realize today that my mom must have had moments when she reflected back on my tests and the doctor's diagnosis and that she was touched by sadness. However, having me home and noting my progress, I know mom was more hopeful and happy.

It was a good vacation. I loved being with the family. I loved my new dog, Shep. We played together constantly during vacation time. But, it was time to go back. The separation never got easier. All the loving touches I experienced from my family will be absent again.

As I grew more, satisfaction came into my life. My vocabulary began to grow. I worked hard to improve my speech and my walking. That growth enabled me to become more helpful to the other children. I was always glad to be able to care for others.

As I said letter reading time continued to be a favorite time. All the children would gather around the teacher and she would read all the letters out loud to all of us kids. One day she called out that the next letter was to me, Benny. It was from my mother. The letter announced bad news. My mom told about my grandfather's sickness and his death. This was the saddest day in my life up to this point. The person, who gave me my first challenge to learn how to walk at 3 ½ years old, and bought me my tractor, was now gone. Playing with my friends and riding my beloved John Deere tractor helped me to deal with my sadness through the day.

Teddy was my best friend at the School. We had a great time together. I was with him all the time. I would get up in the morning and help him dress. He was paralyzed from the neck down. They had to take the back off of his wheel chair and lay a board down so he could ride in the chair. Teddy was an incredible person. He could take notes by picking up a pencil with his mouth and write. He could also draw that way. Teddy and I would play baseball. He would put the bat in his mouth and hit the ball. Then he would roll around the bases on his wheel chair. He was always the pitcher. He would blow the ball out of his mouth. It was amazing. We hung out together a lot.

The picnic in May was always a good time. The fire department in Jamestown came and put on the picnic for us. Hamburgers and hotdogs for everyone! I enjoyed those big fire trucks with ladders. I liked going into the truck and pulling on the siren; I loved that noise. I wanted to be like those guys. That was why I wanted to learn how to undress and dress fast so I could slide down the pole. It was fun to learn about the fire hoses, fire hydrants and how the long ladders worked.

Summer is coming soon and I will be able to go home. I am looking forward to playing outside with my dog Shep and my tractor. Maybe I will get a ride on a real John Deere tractor.

There is a large bulletin board on the wall in the hallway. I check the board to look for my name. I am not on the bulletin board. The names on the bulletin board are those who do not come back in the fall. Does it mean that I have to come back in the fall? I don't want to come back in the fall! Each day I look at the bulletin board to see if my name was there. It is never on the board that spring.

Something happened that helped me feel better about coming back to school in the fall. Also on the bulletin board was an announcement about a "Hoe Down" in the auditorium on Friday night. There were cowboys with bib overalls and bandannas around their necks. They looked like my grandfather who always wore those bib overalls with stripes and big pockets in front. They were sitting on hay bales and singing great songs. It was really fun. However, I discovered they were not real cowboys. They were high school students putting on a show. They came into the audience and introduced themselves to us. Mostly I remember Judy. She was a sophomore or junior in high school. She often came to play her guitar and sing for us. Later she invited me to her church. This was not the regular big church where I walked around and the sermons were long. This place was a tiny church and I enjoyed going there with Judy. She brought me candy and took me downtown to walk around. On Sunday she would take me to have a homemade meal.

I said goodbye to Judy and went home for the summer. "I will see you next fall, Judy." "Yes you will," she said. "We will hang out together when you come back." Her family was so nice to me.

June came and mom and dad took me home for the summer. What a great time I had that summer. I played baseball with my friends. I rode on tractors and combines. Mom and Dad tucked me into my own bed. I played in the dirt. I dug holes and buried things. I hung out with the boys. Everybody was nice to me. I went to Pee Wee baseball games. I took swimming lessons. I didn't have to think about or go to therapy or do classroom stuff. I could play every day and all day. What a great life I had!

The summer went by fast. All too soon it was Labor Day and I had to go back to the Crippled Children's School in Jamestown. Once again I had to say goodbye to my family. But, I had a new friend waiting for me there. I also knew there would be letters, phone calls and, perhaps, a visit.

"Benny, somebody is here to visit you." I ran outside to see who had come. It was my Dad with a big long truck. It had a "combine" on the back of the truck. I don't know if he was coming back from, or going to, the dealer. I only remember hanging out with him for a while. He couldn't stay long because he was working. It was great to see him and I realized I loved him even more than before.

I'm told that I was a very rambunctious, typical boy who liked to play tricks on other kids. Of course, the other kids did some "pay back" to me which I didn't like. I remember one night walking down a dark hallway. A girl jumped out in front of me. She had a hook on her left arm and had only one eye. She was really scary. I don't know what I had done to her. I think we tend to forget that part. She hit me on the top of my head with her hook. It really hurt. That thing was sharp. I think I cried. I sure did not like the "pay back."

There were many ways to keep things exciting. I used to hop on the back of the wheelchairs that had a motor. I loved to ride on machinery. Mom was always trying to figure out why I needed shoes so often. I think I was standing on the battery and the acid made holes in my shoes. My friend Teddy and I were always together and always getting into trouble. I guess we had too much energy. I was one of the few who could walk on my own, so the staff worked extra hard keeping track of me and what I did. I don't think they appreciated the excitement I created.

My high school friend, Judy, continued to visit me and take me downtown.

There were always people coming and going, taking tours of the school. It was one of the most famous schools in the country that served children with disabilities. People came from all over the country to go to school in Jamestown. We had kids from Alaska, Hawaii, California, New York and Maine. I think there were 92 students from all over the country with various disabilities.

Early on at the Crippled Children's School, as a very young boy, I would often see a lady walking on crutches who had no arms. She seemed to be an important person. Often she was leading people on tours through the school. I found out later that these were people like Lawrence Welk, John F. Kennedy and Nelson Rockefeller. To me the lady looked scary, but I knew she had an important job. Her office was in the front part of the school. She turned out to be the superintendent of the school. I tried to be very nice around her because I did not want to have to go to her office. I thought she might hit me over the head with one of her crutches, which, of course, she never did. As I grew older I realized that Dr. Anne Carlsen was the superintendent of the Crippled Children's School. She had been born without any legs and arms. She had achieved a PhD in education and was world famous for her work with children with disabilities. My mother was always amazed at Anne. She often told me the story about being at a banquet with Anne.

She said she watched Anne eating peas. She said Anne was so graceful using her two arm stumps to hold a fork and eat the peas without dropping them. My mother was most grateful to Anne for what she gave me. Mom was terrified by what she had heard at my initial evaluation, but was now grateful for this school and how it gave me a foundation for my future.

It was now the spring of 1965, eight years after I had enrolled. My name was finally on the bulletin board. I would not be coming back next year. I was thrilled to know that I would be home with my family and friends. I did not have to go back to this place I had called home for eight years, from the fall of 1957 until the spring 1965. It was a good place for me, but my life needed to go beyond that place. I was going home to Kenmare to sleep in my own home and eat with my family.

I was recommended to be put into Special Education in my home town of Kenmare, North Dakota.

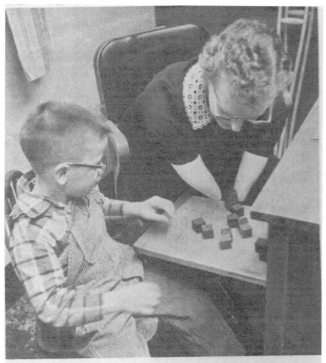

Moving blocks with her stubs, Miss Carlsen gives intelligence tests to children at the school. Pupil here is Benny Anderson of Kenmare, N. D.

Benny at the Crippled Children's School

Benny

26

Chapter Three
"Back At Home"

In the summer of 1965 we took a family vacation to Colorado. It was a good time. I was very excited about being with my family and knowing that I would be going to school in my own town. I did not have to think about Labor Day weekend and leaving the family again. I enjoyed the summer because I could play with my friends most of the time. I especially liked playing baseball. The excitement of being at home was unbelievable.

As autumn rolled around my parents got me ready for my first day of classes. What an exciting time it was for all of us. I was in a small classroom. I was put into a special education class as the Crippled Children's School had recommended. We had a man teacher and he did a lot with us. I remember going on a field trip to Bismarck that spring to tour the state capitol. Everything was going fine for me until the day I began to realize that I was different.

When I began to play outside in the playground with other children at the school, the other kids began to pick on me. I was not used to that kind of ridicule. Before, I had been in school with just kids with disabilities. This was a new chapter in my life and a new environment. I began to feel that I was different and nobody liked me. Nobody wanted to play with me and I was always the last person to be picked for teams. I cried about that a lot. I could not understand why I was being picked on. I had never been treated like that before in my life. All the people at CCS (Crippled Children's School) treated me well and liked me. Why was it different in this school?

I began to realize that I was in a different environment and I needed to adjust to it. I went home crying a lot and my parents felt sorry for me about that. But as time went on people began to get used to my personality, speech and walk. They began to allow me to be the person I was.

As the year progressed I got involved with the

excitement of sports. The Kenmare High School "Honkers" were hot and were winning basketball games right and left. I carried popcorn and soda at the games. That year the "Honkers" took the state championship in basketball. I remember getting up very early in the morning and going down the hall where there was a "Pep Rally." I believe it was two-thirty in the morning. I began to feel that I did belong to the community in spite of being different and still getting picked every so often.

I remember a man who hired me for a dollar to put flyers on car windshields. His name was Elmer C. Johnson. Over the next three or four years, Elmer and I became very good friends. We often took drives and in the fall we went hunting. It was always fun to ride in his old pickup truck. I think my mother told me that she had driven in that same pickup when she was in high school. Elmer enjoyed cooking; on New Year's Eve we would make Swedish meatballs. We also played a lot of cards.

In the fall of 1967 Elmer became the Ward County school superintendent and was an important person in the community. He held that position for thirty-two years and I was glad I was his friend. We called him E.C. He always encouraged me to go beyond my limitations. He took an interest in me and my future. Elmer C. Johnson was one of the great mentors in my life. I learned a lot from him as our friendship went on. He reminded me that I was bigger than my disability and that I needed to further my education to fulfill my dreams. He embraced my dreams. Elmer was truly a person who helped shape my career as a person with a disability.

A number of years later when I was in High School I was told that I needed to pass a driver's education class in order to graduate. And I said, "No I don't!" That Friday morning I mentioned it to Mr. Johnson. That same day my teacher received a phone call from E. C. Johnson. I didn't need to take the driver's education class after all. (I really would never be able to drive because of my disability.) My teacher was taken aback by that phone call because I had used my influence.

I did a lot that first year back at home. It was a tough time but I was thankful to be home with my parents and friends. I finally felt a part of the community.

At the same time the special education experience was frustrating for me. I had dreams; I had ideas. I wanted to go beyond my disability but I felt trapped inside. I was always haunted by my low IQ label and struggled with everything related to that label. Why did I need to go through this crap? I wanted to go to college, to be someone great. I wanted to be a writer, or a minister. I wanted to be recognized. I don't belong in this special education class! Why don't people understand that I have a lot more ahead of me than they can see? I thought, "why can E.C. see my potential, but nobody else can?"

I took long walks through the prairie grasses and thought about my future. I got away from all the misconceptions of who I was. I began to dream about my life, the perfect life that I would have. But how could I break out of this mess I was in? My frustrations became so intense that I acted up in school one day. I took my math book and ripped it to pieces. Guess what my homework was for the next three days? You got it! Mom and Dad bought some scotch tape and told me that this was not the kind of behavior that would be acceptable. I understood that. But I am not sure they understood the level of my frustration.

School was very different from what I was used to at the CCS. I was at the Kenmare School for two years. Then my third year I attended school in Minot. I went to Junior High and was in the Special Ed. Program. I lived with a family in Minot, but that did not work out and I moved in with a family that I had known in Kenmare and that worked out fine. I went to Ramstad Junior High in Minot for one year.

The next year I was to go to high school in Minot. I lived at home and took a bus each day from Kenmare to Minot. I would leave at 7 o'clock in the morning and get to Minot by 8:30 am. I would leave school on the bus at 3:00 pm and arrive home at 5:00 pm. Every day on the bus was the same. What can you say about riding on the same bus with the same people you were with all day in school in the same Special Ed class? We had about five stops to pick up other students on the way to Minot.

As a teenager I always wanted to have a relationship with a girl. I wondered, "Could I find a girl who would accept me the way I am? Could she accept the way I speak? Could she accept the way I walk? Could she look beyond my disability and see me as a real person?"

As a junior in high school I began to date a girl who was also in Special Ed. Her name was Nancy. Nancy was born eighty-five percent deaf. That year Nancy and I went to the Prom together. Of course, my parents had to take me since I did not drive. It was hard to have a date for the Prom and have your parents as a chaperone. However, life could have been a lot worse. At least I had a date. My desires to have someone care for me came true. Nancy and I dated for the next year and a half.

One of the funniest stories about our relationship occurred over a phone call. Remember that Nancy was eighty-five percent deaf, so her hearing was not always accurate. I called her to tell her that I was going to Wahpeton Science School for five weeks for a special class. I received a letter from her later and it was clear that she did not hear what I had been saying. She thought I was going to be going out with someone else and dumping her. It took some doing to straighten out the situation. I realized that phone calls were not the best way to communicate with her. We continued to date through my senior year in high school. That summer we went our separate ways. What a journey that was. Even though our breaking up broke my heart, I can say that I dated in high school.

Those were the years I traveled by bus to Minot, three years of special education. The days were long but I had my dreams of the future to help me stay energized and alive. I had a part time job in a sheltered workshop in Minot. It was something different from school but I knew that I did not have a future in the workshop. I knew also that I wanted to go to college but I was in Special Ed. And they told me that I had this low IQ. I was in Special Ed. but I knew that I did not belong there.

I was so frustrated. How can I ever get out of this trap? I had so many people telling me what I should do with my life, but nobody ever listened to what I said about my life. That situation created a great deal of anger and frustration in me. Again, I took long walks in the country and dreamed about my future. I was trying to find a graceful way to get out of the situation I was in. So many thoughts were raising questions. Why should I be riding this bus and going to a special education classroom? Why am I here? Who is in charge of this? Surely, it is not I.

One day a dramatic turn of events happened. A Doctor in the Special Education Department at Minot State told me that there had been a mistake. I was not mentally retarded or slow. I should not be in special education. I should have been in regular school. I was a junior at the time with one year left in special education. I thought to myself, "Now you get it but it is too late." I told them that I thought it was too late. The end of schooling was in sight and I was in no way prepared for a senior year in regular high school. It would be like "putting someone into deep water who did not know how to swim." I chose not to go into a regular high school classroom. I graduated from high school on the 24th day of May, in 1972. I received a "certificate of completion" from special education.

That summer I worked for the Kenmare Public School with my father. I mowed a lot of grass and helped with a lot of other tasks. I also hung out with my friends and went fishing often. The questions about my future were still on my mind. What was I going to do with the rest of my life? I had dreams and desires but how would they come true?

Fall came and I had to do something. I moved away from home and went to Jamestown, North Dakota where the Crippled Children's School was located. It was a community I knew. I got a job as a dishwasher at the college in town. I made a lot of friends while I was living on campus. I re-connected with my friend Judy and her family who had been so good to me while I was at the school. While there I came to realize that I was not going to be a dishwasher the rest of my life. I wondered which of my dreams would come true. Would I write books? Would I be a speaker? As I thought about these dreams I pondered my ongoing question, "How is this going to happen?"

1974

Chapter Four
"Trying To Fly"

I quit my job as a dishwasher, which meant that I would have to move home with my family. It was a long winter for my folks and for me. Early in the Spring I left home and went back to Jamestown and got my old job back as a dishwasher at the college. That fall an opportunity came to me to move to Grand Forks, North Dakota but I was stuck back in a sheltered workshop again. I really did not want to be there. It was another one of those frustrating times in my life. Once again my dreams were on hold and seemed so far away from being fulfilled. I got through this time in my life but I did not enjoy it. I always seemed to be able to survive even the worst nightmares.

Later that fall I moved to the West Coast to be involved in a treatment program called "creep and crawl." This method attempted to re-train the brain from one side to the other. I was there for seven months. While there I received a letter from a friend of mine from Grand Forks who asked me to come back and live there. In the letter he challenged me to accept my disability and become comfortable with it. As I meditated on that letter something clicked in my mind. I began to realize that my disability was going to be the catalyst of my career.

That Christmas I went home to my family knowing I was not going to go back to the West Coast for those treatments. After Christmas I went back to Grand Forks to live. One Sunday morning I went to church. It was a typical worship Service. After the Service a guy came up to me and introduced himself. His name was Wayne Nelson. He wanted to come to visit me in my home. I was curious as to what he wanted since he gave me no clues as to the purpose of his visit. I invited him to come. I waited for his visit with great curiosity. He came. I answered the knock on the door and let him in. I could hardly believe what he was saying to me. He wanted me to work with him to develop a program of speaking to schools and churches about issues related to people with disabilities. My own disability and life experience was to be the catalyst for my involvement in this program. It seemed that he knew everything I had been thinking about in my dreams and conversations with myself.

For the next five to six months I spoke in schools and churches about relating to people with disabilities and the struggle they had in being accepted and affirmed. I had an office and put together a board to direct this work. I was going to meetings and making decisions. Finally, I had gotten out of the trap. By the grace of God this man had come out of nowhere and enabled me to become a partner in his work. How did he know what I had been dreaming? How did he know that I could do this? It was a great time for me. He was like Elmer C. Johnson. Wayne encouraged me to be who I wanted to be. He encouraged me to go beyond what I, and others thought, were limitations because of my disability. What a great gift these two men gave me.

Then, one day, Wayne called me and said that the grant funding for this program had run out. It was a sad day. We closed the office and dismissed the board. Once again my dreams were put on hold.

Earlier that year I had made application to the University of North Dakota. I had not heard from the University yet. It was summer and I had lost my job. As I was finishing up the last bit of work for Wayne, a phone call came inviting me to interview for a summer job at Red Willow Bible Camp. The interview went well and I was hired for the summer. It was a great summer. I enjoyed working with young people. However, I had no clue as to what I might be doing in the fall. I still had not heard from the University. It had been seven months since I applied. During the last weeks at the camp I finally heard from the school that I was not accepted. They did not accept my transcript from high school because it was not a diploma but a "certificate of completion" of special education. Why did they bother to give me this piece of paper that would not be recognized by the board of education of North Dakota? Also, I scored very low on my ACT test. I expected that because I was in special education. I did not have much grounding in grammar, math and reading. I remember taking the test as it was read to me. I believe I received a score of 6. It was probably one of the lowest scores in the country.

I had become used to adversity in my life. I was not going to let that letter deny me my dreams of going to college. As I stared at that letter of denial I thought about my next step. Time was running out. The beginning of school was coming soon. I made a phone call to one of my best friends. He was a lawyer. He was very acquainted with my situation. I told him that I had received a denial from the university. He said he was very sorry about that news. He knew how much I wanted to go to school, especially at University of North Dakota, since many of my friends were there. He told me it would be difficult to mediate this situation since there was so little time. He said that we could fight the university on this issue but it seemed doubtful to him that we could win. Then he said, "Let me see what I can do for you." The next week I received a call from him telling me that he had talked to someone at Lake

Region Junior College in Devil's Lake, North Dakota. The next week I received an acceptance letter from them. Everything seemed to be back on track. In three weeks I would be in college.

There I was in college. I began to wonder if I could do it. My wondering turned to conviction. I was going to do it! I registered for six credits. At first it was nerve racking, but gradually I adjusted to college life. The only thing I did not like was homework. I would rather socialize. Friends were very important to me. Two high school friends I had met at the camp where I worked for the summer lived nearby. I did a lot with them on the weekends. One weekend they invited me to a concert at their church. A team of young adults gave a concert and shared their faith stories. They talked about singing and speaking at many places across the country. I thought this would be a great summer job for me. I picked up an application and sent it in to the organization.

That spring I did receive a letter of invitation from Lutheran Youth Encounter to spend the summer on a team.

The first year of college was enjoyable but very difficult since I did not have much high school preparation for college. My classes went fairly well in spite of that preparation. I enjoyed being at the junior college but felt that I would rather go to a private church related college.

1978

Chapter Five
"Living My Dream"

I reached a point in my life where I focused my hopes on three dreams. The first was to develop an organization that would advocate for persons of disability. Secondly, I would go to college. Thirdly, I would write a book.

The application that I received from the Lutheran Youth Encounter organization would enable me to take a big step if I was accepted for a team. I thought it would give me a chance to break out and begin my dreams. I remember asking myself a question as I filled out the application. Why was I thinking I would be denied? At times my confidence was not very strong. I had too many hopes that had been shattered over the years. I was surprised when I received a letter of call saying that I was accepted to come to St. Paul to join college students from all over the country to spend the summer speaking and singing.

My mother was very nervous that day that she put me on a plane to St. Paul. I was going to be in a big city, a city much bigger than the little town I was from. It was a big city, where lights and noise and excitement were all around. It certainly was not like the playground in Kenmare, N.D. that I had enjoyed so much.

I met many new people who would become my co-workers and friends as we gathered for team training. Two men, in particular, were very helpful to me - Loren Teig and Joel Sunde. They continue to be good friends to me. Loren was the director of the teams. He was the person from whom I received the letter of acceptance to join the summer staff. Joel was a regional director for the area I was working in.

Training was somewhat like college. There were a lot of lectures and a lot of conversation about relationships with youth. Lutheran Youth Encounter is an organization that works with churches to encourage young people to be involved in the church's life and ministry. I was excited to be a part of the organization that had sent a team to North Dakota to make a connection for me to be a part of this adventure.

I was assigned to be on an inner city team. Four of us worked together as a team in an inner city church in downtown Minneapolis. One night during the first week at the church I went for a walk by myself. The neighborhood was not totally safe. I should not have gone by myself but I was a country boy used to going for walks at night. Two men approached me and I began to get nervous and shake in my boots (even though I did not have any boots on). I did not want to get robbed. They took me back to where I was living and I thought that was strange. They did not do anything to me but I was shaken up in anticipation of what might happen. That night I did not know what to do. Pastor Berg who was my supervisor came in to talk to me and I told him what had happened. He asked me if I wanted to go home. I told him I did not want to go home.

The next week the strangest thing happened to me again. Those two men came up to me again as we were eating at our weekly dinner together at the church. They apologized to me and said they were sorry for what they had done. It took me aback and at the same time taught me something about forgiveness. We fed them that night at the banquet.
I had a lot to learn. I was a farm boy from a small town. I did not even know how to do the laundry. The girls on the team refused to wait on me hand and foot. Loren Teig showed me how to wash clothes.

I learned a lot that summer, not only about myself, but about how the church should interact with people who are oppressed. As the summer wore on I began to think about what my next move should be. I was riding a city bus one day when I came up with the thought that I should make contact with a private college nearby. I really should get back to school. I called the school and went to meet a person in the admissions office. We went out for coffee and he showed me around the campus. I had no idea what it would cost. I remember my mother saying that it was nice that I wanted to go to a private Lutheran college, but she soon found out it was going to cost twice as much as Lakes Region Junior college.

That fall I enrolled as a special student at Golden Valley Lutheran College. I was living on campus and took eight credits. I was put on academic probation until the second week when I met with my advisor. He took me off probation when he saw the grades I received on my tests and assignments. Golden Valley was more challenging than Lake Regions. I had much more reading to do. I was not a good reader. I spent a year and a half at Golden Valley College. I went home at Christmas time to be with my family. My minister at home talked to me and encouraged me to apply for a job at the national office of the Lutheran Church. I did call and show interest in the position.

After Christmas I returned to Golden Valley. At the beginning of the new quarter at school I realized I was not going to be able to finish my work. At the same time I received a notice for an interview with the American Lutheran Church for the job that was open. I was nervous at the interview but was excited about the job because it fit my interests and concerns. After the interview I realized that the job was much bigger than I was. I did not get the job.

For some odd reason, as I was leaving the church offices of the American Lutheran Church, I stopped to talk to a gentleman, the Rev. Dick Beckmen. He was Director of youth ministries and the Luther League. After realizing that I was not going to get the job for which I had interviewed, I went to Dick and shared my dream of starting a non-profit organization for education and advocacy on behalf of people with disabilities.

In March of 1978 I made my first presentation as the Director of Break Through. One night, at a board meeting of Break Through, I announced that I wanted to write a book. Dick Beckmen volunteered to help me.

One day I was on campus in my office at Golden Valley Lutheran College. I left and walked down the hallway. I met a young woman in the hall. I invited her to have a cup of coffee. Her name was Joan. We began to hang out together after that. At one point we had one of the longest phone calls I had ever had in my life. We talked for two and a half hours. I don't remember what we talked about or who called whom. Our relationship grew that summer. In the fall I was back on the road speaking and Joan was back in school. We had talked about getting engaged but we both seemed very busy and focused on our work and school. That fall, on the anniversary of our meeting the first time, I was to be in Chicago at a meeting. I called Joan and arranged for her to go out for dinner at a fine restaurant. I also arranged for someone to take her flowers for me.   Unknown to Joan I was actually in Minneapolis. I arrived at the restaurant while she was eating. She was quite surprised because I had called her and said I was in Chicago. We often laughed about that evening. We eventually got engaged. That Christmas we took the train to North

Dakota so she could meet my parents. We spent a few days there. We returned to Minneapolis to take part in a youth convention. We also spent New Year's Eve together. Shortly after that we broke up our relationship. There were several complications including my lack of confidence in my ability to support her and a family. We both came to that agreement. It was painful. We had spent a year and a half together.

Dick and I did write a book together called, "Breaking Through". I remember the many days we spent writing it together over lunch. Dick and I seemed to forget paper and our notes were written on paper napkins. It was amazing that Dick could decipher the script with all the "pizza sauce" on them. That was a great time. It was a book about my disability and my faith.

As I traveled and spoke I began to realize that my dreams were coming true. I accomplished many things. I have gone beyond the expectations of others. But, my college dream is still out there. I tried college in several places but it did not work out for me. I still believed I could do it if I tried hard enough once again.

I took a class in English Comprehension at the Minneapolis Community College. I did very well in the class. It was a great encouragement to me to be able to succeed at last in a college class.

The next summer was another interesting episode in finding a relationship. I met a girl at a retreat and fell in love with her. She was from a small town in Iowa. I was happy to have a relationship again. Patty had cerebral palsy. She held a Masters degree in social work. The relationship did not last very long. Again, sadness was experienced. I was working and living my dream and she was living far away from me. I felt I could not move since my organization, Break Through, was beginning to "take off" and things were moving well.

Among my travels I found myself in Kansas City at a disability conference. I don't remember much about the content of the conference. One evening I met a couple at the conference who invited me to have lunch with them the next day. They were the parents of a girl that was born with cerebral palsy and other disabilities. It was supposed to be lunch date but turned out to be three hours of conversation. I was intrigued by their story of caring for their daughter. They were amazing parents. This was the beginning of a long friendship with Tom and Harriet Rose. The next February they invited me to spend a week at their home. I met their daughter, Nancy, who was a teenager at the time.

The conversations with Harriet and Tom were invaluable. They had so much to offer and many insights to share. My experience growing up and their experience of caring for Nancy complemented each other. This was in the early days of developing my organization and information that the Rose's shared was among the best education I could have received. For me to be able to come and be a part of this family's life enabled me to see many new issues and ways of responding to the needs of someone like

Nancy. The daily activities of taking care of a person with severe disabilities can be demanding and complex. I realized later in my career that this event had helped me personally and professionally a great deal in understanding family dynamics in this kind of a situation.

In the back of my mind I knew I needed to go back to college. The obstacle was that I was having too much fun. I was speaking at conferences, traveling across the country and hanging out with people like the Rose family. However there was something lacking. My dream to write a book was completed. The non-profit organization was put together. The dream of finishing college was still out there. Lake Region Junior College was fine, but difficult. Golden Valley was OK. I enjoyed taking the class at Minneapolis Community College. I thought that maybe it was time to try again. I decided that I would enroll at Augsburg College in Minneapolis. I could go to school and travel to conferences on the weekend. I enrolled at Augsburg but found it frustrating. I always say that I went to Augsburg for three weeks and it cost me three hundred dollars. I took two classes. One was Political Science. That required a lot of reading and I could not keep up. The other class was Biology. We studied the human body and it all seemed like another language to me. I remember asking the question, "What is an atom?" Everyone in class stopped what they were doing and looked at me. I knew what they were thinking. The professor said that I should stop by his office that night. I knew I was in trouble. I was right! I was in trouble. I was dropped from school. Well, this was the fourth time I left the hallowed halls of academia. I had a hard time believing that it was really happening to me again.

In the spring of 1988 I found myself lost. I was not making very much money. My life was not headed in any real direction. I went to Lake Wapogasset Lutheran Bible Camp in Amery, Wisconsin. I was going to look for a job in that area. Jerry, a friend of mine in the local news office, somehow knew of my situation which he had explained to another person. They recommended that I explore the college in Menomonie, Wisconsin. The following Monday my

58

friend Paul and I found ourselves signing me up for the fall semester. I remember thinking that I had to make this happen. But, somehow it had to be a different way this time.

Graduation-1992-UW-Stout

Chapter Six
"Getting my Degree"

I was looking forward with excitement as I was about to launch another attempt at attending college. I was also nervous as I remembered the times in the past when I was asked to leave school because I was not able to keep up with my work. I was trying to stay positive in my thinking. I recommitted myself to the task. I had to make my best attempt! In spite of the long journey that lay ahead of me I enrolled in school in September of 1988. I began my classes after Labor Day and moved into the dormitory room on campus. I lived in the dorm for a year and a half. It was a mixed blessing. I was close to everything on campus but I did not like dorm life. I was stuck in this tiny room and it reminded me of when I was 18 years old and being at Lake Regions Junior College. I knew what dorm life was like and it got old fast. Eventually I got out of there. For the last two and a half years I lived off campus in an apartment.

My major study area was Vocational Rehabilitation. VR had always been rough on me. They never gave me credit for high school. They never helped me get to college. I had always had bad feelings for VR. This created an interesting dilemma. I had very negative feelings about what they had done to me in the past, but now I am devoting my life to that very thing.

Normally I would have been a part time student. However, I decided to take a full load of 12 credits. This meant I had to be more intensive in my study and pay attention to my schedule. How was I going to do this? It dawned on me that I needed to set up a support system. I needed others to help me write papers and take notes in class.

This was a different approach for me. When I went to college before, I tried to do it all on my own. Because of my zeal to succeed and to prove myself, I failed. I realized that did not work for me. I needed assistance.

I began to look around and search out resources for this task. I went to one office and then another, asking people to point to the resources I needed. Finally, I took it upon myself to handpick the people I could use to help me. I developed good relationships with the people in my support system. This "community of people" was going to be an important part of my college career. They were going to help me be a successful student. If I were to fail, it would not be their fault. It would be my problem. This arrangement meant that I had to schedule all my assignments according to my support teams' schedule.

As time went on the support system became more and more important to me. I became more familiar with my workload and what was required of me as a student. I did have a lot of fun in the midst of this academic challenge. There was time to go out and play.

I had to take a lot of classes that dealt with rehabilitation. They were very informational classes. I learned a lot about attitudes toward folks that had disabilities. I also gained important information about people with various disabilities. I also took some classes outside of the rehab department. That was not recommended by my program director but I took them anyway. I was interested in those subjects. At one point the director was concerned that I would not graduate in time because I was taking these other classes outside the department. I felt the real reason was that the department was not getting the money for those classes. My concern was to get more of a rounded education. I wanted to be a well-informed person and not limited to just one concern. I did finish on time with my degree work.

One of the hardest classes for me emotionally was learning about re-evaluation. I went in to class one day and found myself learning about IQ tests and how they were administered. I began to feel a sadness and also an anger rising up in me. I tried to figure out why that sort of mood was taking over my mind. I was always such an upbeat person. But, then I began crying a lot. I realized that I was thinking back to my childhood and the misdiagnosis that happened to me. All of the memories of how much that affected my life negatively flooded over me. Now, here I was learning how to be a professional and engage in diagnosis.

This event triggered a profound response on my part. I entered counseling on a long term basis to help me sort out my feelings about being misdiagnosed and how these feelings were affecting the person that I was. This was a difficult time for me. It was like being in a movie that I was playing a part in. It took several months for us to be able to sort that out. I am so glad that I sought out help at that point in my life. I am a better and stronger person because I did go for counseling. This was another lesson for me to not go it alone.

That experience was an important part of my self education and self development. It helped me to look at the emotions of one person's misdiagnosis of a low IQ and all the psychological impact that came from it. What an opportunity to examine this whole issue from the inside of my own experience. It was a different kind of learning experience. I became the textbook. Some people may have thought that I was weak because I needed so much help. Actually, I was strong because I did reach out for help in spite of what people may have thought about me.

Each year at the university raised some of the same questions I always had. It did not get any easier. In fact, each year was harder. Could I really do it? The answer to that was yes. However, I did not know that answer until each year was ended. I discovered that the support system I had set up was enabling me to accomplish this. I was able to maintain a "B" average. Not bad for one diagnosed as a boy with an IQ in the low sixties!

It came time to take a course in physiology. I was dreading this class because of my previous experience at Augsburg College, when I was asked to drop out because I revealed my lack of learning by asking what an atom was. I needed to get a "C" in this class because it was one of the core courses in my major. Actually, I had to take both physiology and physiology of the disabled. I had my work cut out for me.

My support system had a wonderful note taker who got everything written down that I needed to learn. In addition, my tutor was the best, my instructor. This happened in an interesting way. I did not do very well in my first test. The instructor suggested I get a tutor. I asked him to recommend one for me. He said he would recommend the best one he knew. When I asked what the name of the tutor was, he said, "Me!" He also said that if I promised to work hard he would meet with me twice a week. I told him that I would do my very best, and I did. I did get through the two courses. These were the most challenging courses I had to take. I had received very little preparation for science classes in my special education classes in high school. The assumption at that time was that I would never need that kind of information. I worked hard and received a passing grade. It was a high "C."

A similar situation occurred in a math class that I was required to take. My first test paper came back with an upside down "A" at the top of the page. I was in trouble again. I had never experienced this level of math before. But again I was able to get through this class with some intense tutoring sessions and a very understanding instructor.

I had another experience that helped with my development. I was appointed to the Stout Student Association - University Student Senate as an off-campus senator. This was during the first year I lived off campus. I was voted to a second term year as well. The Senate was interesting. We dealt with behavioral problems on campus. We had to keep in mind the welfare of the entire campus community. My being on the senate taught me much about government and how to get things done in a proper way. I had no idea what the Robert's Rules of Order were. I started out with always being called out of order. It got so bad they finally gave me a copy of Robert's Rules of Order to read. I did not understand why we had to be so formal.

The Senate also provided another opportunity for me to grow. I was asked to address the state gathering of the Wisconsin State Senate when they met on our campus. I was asked to speak to them about ADA (American Disabilities Act) and other related areas that people with disabilities face on campus.

During my last semester I went on internship. Pinckney Hall was my supervisor. I took my internship at the counseling center at the university. I was the first undergraduate student to do their internship on campus. My concentration area was psychological testing.

When the semester was over I stayed on for a month to assist in the planning and implementation of a psychological conference This conference planning was a great learning experience. I was responsible for coordinating various pieces of the conference. I also enjoyed the interaction with professionals from all parts of Wisconsin.

Pinckney Hall, who was my intern supervisor, became my friend as well. He also became involved as a volunteer in my organization, Break Through Inc. after I graduated. Pinckney had a unique way of understanding who I was and my dreams and struggles. He was the supervisor of those who counseled with me when I was having my struggles in school. I am very thankful for him and the assistance he gave me on the difficult but great journey through college.

In August of 1992 I received my Bachelor's Degree in Vocational Rehabilitation with an emphasis on community based rehab. I finished with a grade point average of 3.29. Not bad for being told that I was not capable of going to college. What a joy it was to be able to entertain my parents and other friends who came to my graduation. It was the most wonderful day in my life up to that point. I had accomplished my third goal before I was 40 years old. The university journey was a hard journey, much like the journey that began back in my "20's" when I was at Lake Region Junior College. Or perhaps the journey really began in my boyhood days as I dreamed of succeeding to become somebody important. Or, maybe the journey really began when I was a little tyke and my grandfather challenged me to learn to walk, promising to get me that little green John Deere pedal tractor when I did.

Now I was holding in my hand a degree from a university. As I looked back from that day, I realized that I could not have done this by myself. There were many people who challenged, encouraged and assisted me from the beginning to this point. My heart is grateful to my parents who never gave up on who I was and what my dreams were. A countless number of people were there during the achievement of each of my three major goals. Many of these people continue to be an important part of my life as the journey goes on.

Overcoming, obstacles and reaching out to the world

BREAKING THROUGH

By Ben D. Anderson
and Dick Beckmen

Chapter Seven
"Go for it!"

As a child we use our imagination to dream wonderful dreams. Often we are asked to go out and play with invisible toys. Nothing was impossible in most of our play. I had a great imagination. I was always walking by myself with something in my hand. It may have been a stick. But I could imagine that stick being a crutch or a rod. I could be in a pile of dirt digging a hole with my toys and imaging all sorts of construction projects.

When I was a boy my family had moved to town from the country. I really did not like it in town. I enjoyed the country and missed it very much. In the country we lived by a big coulee. I liked to play in that coulee. I wanted to build a tunnel between the coulee and my bedroom. I used my road grader, my crane and my trucks to build that road. I pretended that I was a big construction company. I was going to build this long tunnel and then open the side of the house and let the road run into my bedroom. That was my kind of imagination.

On another occasion my father came up to me while I was digging a deep hole. He asked me why I was digging it. I said that I was mad. He asked me who I was mad at. I told him that I was mad at the devil. I also had a hammer in my hand. He asked about the hammer. I replied that when I get this hole deep enough to see the devil, I am going to hit him over the head with this hammer. My father snickered and said, "keep on digging."

Children have imaginations. The imagination can turn into a dream and dreams can turn into realities. That happened to me when I took long walks in the country. I would begin to imagine what I would be when I grew up. I had dreams that included seeing myself as a great person doing great things at some point in time. I did not accept the notion that I had a low IQ. I didn't know what a low IQ really meant, but I know that I didn't accept what people said about me. I had my dreams and I knew I would get there some day.

We were told to use our imaginations as children. I don't understand what happens but I was told that we lose our imaginations when we get older. Maybe it is because we begin to look at how difficult some things are. Or, we see too many of these difficulties as roadblocks rather than possibilities that can challenge us to go beyond. We loose the sense that the impossible can be possible. Often we get frustrated because things seem so hard and impossible. Often we take the easy way out and drop our dreams. How many dreams have you had that you did not follow through with them because you thought they were impossible?

I am told that I am a person that does not give up. I am very consistent. Once I lock onto a dream I follow through. I had three big dreams in my mind and I committed myself to complete all three. It took a lot of work and many other people helping me on these dream journeys.

Those journeys were not easy. But I was bound and determined not to give them up. I kept my childhood ventures of digging that tunnel or digging to find the devil alive. That determination stayed with me. Some may call that stubbornness. Maybe it is like that. I prefer to call it passion for a dream.

Now I am an adult and that passion is still in me. As an adult I do have the capabilities to put my dreams into action. They have not been simple or easy to bring about but they are alive and well.

My first dream was to build an organization. In 1978 I called a group of people together to make up a board of directors. I had no experience in putting an organization together. I thought I could pattern it after groups that I had observed or have been a part of. I had the basic vision and sense about putting this organization together. It took many people to stand behind me and work with me to make it happen.
Today Break Through Inc. is stronger than ever as I continue to live with the same vision and energy as

when I began in 1978. We are working with people throughout the United States.

I began by working with parents of children with disabilities. My first conversation with the Rose family was back in 1980's. That conversation was important to set the pattern of the work that continues today. We are continually working with parent groups.

This dream of beginning a non-profit organization was to me the biggest thing I was going to do. I remember the day I received that letter from my friend asking me to come back to Grand Forks, North Dakota. In that letter he said that my disability was not my worst enemy. When I came back to work with Wayne Nelson I realized that I could begin Break Through and use my disability as my message. It would not only help other people but would help build my confidence in who I am.

I remember when I was back home visiting with E.C. Johnson and the conversation we had about my going back to school. He said that I was bigger than my disability and that my dreams were important. Other people in my life also said, "go for it." My mother was a fine example for me of what it means to "go for it." I still tell myself, "if I can imagine digging a tunnel and digging a hole deep enough to hit the devil on the head with a hammer, I can do this."

I am living my dream. Every presentation I give, every encounter I have with people as an advocate, makes me realize how important that letter was. My disability was not my enemy and it could be my friend. I thank God for that message.

Dreams are still happening. They are like being on a journey that keeps unfolding. Every stop you make on the journey allows something new to come to light. As I travel I meet new people and new situations that create new dreams. These dreams lead on to what is next on this journey. Many doors have opened that have allowed me to serve on boards, committees and projects outside of my organization. This has been a wonderful affirmation of my life vision and purpose.

Of course I got married!

Ben and Dee-3-26-2006

Chapter Eight
"Of course I got married!"

Whoever said the impossible would be possible. I had said that I would not get married. I laughed as I said that but down deep inside I wanted somebody to grow old with. I had been in relationships before but my track record was not very good. They just did not seem to work out or I got cold feet and left. Getting old by myself was a difficult thought for me to come to terms with. It wasn't that I was jealous of my friends that were married. It was the idea of growing old by myself. At that point in my life I was not ready to settle down but someday I knew I would want a companion. Relationships were not working out for me when I was younger. I always imagined that you had to have some sort of wealth in your background to support someone. I guess I never realized that it takes both parties in a relationship to make that financial commitment.

I kept busy doing all sorts of volunteer work once I had moved to Amery, Wisconsin. I especially liked working with my friends at Lake Wapogasset Bible Camp. I helped out with various projects there. There was a lot to do at a place where I spent many summers. I often spoke to young people concerning their life being lived out of a Christian context.

My friends at Lake Wapogasset are still very important to me. I have a sense of family when I am with them. I met most of these people in 1970's. It was the summer I left the Lutheran Youth Encounter team and joined the staff at the camp for the first time. My relationship with the camp staff was very important to me. I had such a sense of belonging with these folks. A sense of having a relationship with one person never really came up as I was always busy with my group of friends.

It was in late fall of 2003 that Joel and I and others were working on the annual Christmas Dinner Theater at Wapogasset. Joel asked me to take this "young lady" over to Paul the manager of the camp.

She had told Joel that she wanted to do some volunteer work on the new building. I did as he asked and took her to meet Paul. Her name was Dee.

About five months later life took an interesting turn. I felt myself being inspired to get to know her a little better. As time went on we got to know each other. We started doing things together. We both enjoyed dancing. I remember one night when we went dancing and I forgot my belt for my pants. When we got up to dance I had to put my hand in the belt loops in the back of my pants to hold them up. Have you ever tried to dance and hold your pants up at the same time? Dee and I laughed and laughed. It really wasn't that bad but it was funny.

We loved to walk and tell stories out in the country where she was living. I could go on talking forever with a straight face, but when it was Dee's turn to tell a story she never could keep a straight face. She giggled through every sentence.

One day we took a ride on an Italian Surrey bike. As you might guess I cannot balance myself on a bike because of my disability. It was a crazy looking bike but it worked. I told Dee that I wanted to buy one but the price was too high for me. Laughing, she asked me how many I wanted.

We did a lot of activities together that fall. I began having feelings for Dee, more than being just a friend. I knew that she only wanted to be my friend. She had told me this many times. One day as we were walking in Dee's favorite place to walk, I asked her to marry me. Of course she thought I was crazy because she had never thought of getting married in her whole life. She considered herself an "old maid" and that time had just passed her by. I realized I had to give her some time to consider the question and I did. Neither of us had been married before.

About three weeks went by and then we went walking in the same place where I had "popped" the question. She said "yes!" We began to make plans for a March wedding. We both agreed that camp Wapogasset would be the place. That Thanksgiving of 2005 Dee and I went to North Dakota so that she could meet my family.

I received an email from a friend of mine in Montana whom I had told about the wedding. In the email he said that if it had been a few years earlier he would have sent Dee his sympathies. But he said that he had finally grown up and would send only congratulations. We had a good laugh about that.

During this busy time I was appointed to sit on the Rehabilitation Council of the state of Wisconsin by the Governor. The first meeting would be the last week of April after we got married.

It was a busy beginning of the year 2006. We got serious about planning for a March 26th wedding. The perfect place for our wedding at Camp Wapogasset would be Anderson Hall. Anderson Hall was named after three Andersons and I was one of them. Dee thought it would be a sentimental and perfect place to get married. I had a lot of friends and family that would be there. Dee came from a small family. As we began to put the guest list together we wondered if Anderson Hall would be big enough. It was.

The day we got married was a beautiful March day. We had a half a foot of snow the week before so there was still snow on the ground but the temperature was very nice. There were about 80 people at the ceremony and another 50 at the reception. I was thrilled to have most of my family there – my parents, Marlys and Russell, my sister Terri and her husband Ronnie as well as two aunts and some cousins.

There were a couple of nice surprises for me. Judy, my volunteer big sister who helped me when I was in the Crippled Children's School in Jamestown, came to the wedding ceremony. I had not seen her for forty years. Steve, who had been my roommate between my junior and senior years in high school, came as well. We had been at summer school together at Wahpeton Science School. I had not seen him for many years. It was so good to see him. Guys that I had hung out together with in high school from

Kenmare came. What a surprise! My best man was Joel who I had met the first summer I was on a Lutheran Youth Encounter team. My second cousin, Dave and Paul whom I had met in the 70's were also in the wedding party. I was waiting for some craziness to happen, but they were all gentlemen, and that was surprising! Dee's wedding party was also quite sane.

During the ceremony I was very emotional. Pastor Barry asked me what token I had brought to the wedding. I was totally blank. He saw the expression on my face and immediately said, Oh, the "ring." Joel, the best man, dug the ring out of his pocket and handed it to me. I began to lighten up and relax as the wedding guests laughed. My anxious emotions left and I was in a good mood for the rest of the ceremony.

It was now official, Dee and I were married on March 26, 2006 at 4:00 pm at Lake Wapogasset Bible camp in Anderson Hall by the Reverend Barry Schaefer and the Reverend Dick Beckmen.

Dee was very shrewd. She parked our car way in the back of the camp so that no one would be able to find it and mess it up. Nobody knew where the car was so there were no surprises. We knew that we had been spared from some trickery because we saw some things lying around that could only be used for messing up a car. I think it could have been my new brother-in-law. I saw him with something in his hand as he was searching around the camp. He didn't find the car. His sister out tricked him!

Dee and I began our life together by taking a month and a half of "honeymoon." We went to Las Vegas and also did a side trip to Hoover Dam. Quite incredible. The scenery had us in awe as we took the tour bus and paddleboat ride on Lake Mead. On the return trip we had a long wait at the airport. Sitting in the waiting area I asked Dee if her wedding ring was comfortable on her hand. She put up her hand and there was no ring on it. That took me aback. I was trying to remember what might have happened to her ring. Then I realized she was playing a trick on me as she had lifted up her right hand and not her left hand with the ring on it! I was so tired it took me a few moments to realize what she did. Of course she started to giggle. Of course! Then I knew. Married life was going to be full of surprises and fun.

We came home but did not stay there very long. My first meeting of the State Rehabilitation Council was being held in Milwaukee. So we were off again. Our honeymoon continued. We traveled by car and saw some beautiful country as we extended our trip to include Illinois, Kansas and Missouri as well as Wisconsin. It was a great beginning to what we hoped would be a long life together.

Dee has joined me in the advocacy program I began in 1978. She has become an important part of the organization. We will continue together to educate people about disabilities. Dee and I have made our home in a small town in Wisconsin. We are both involved in our community.

Today I look back on the time that I realized I did not want to get old by myself. I am so thankful that this woman that I met at Lake Wapogasset married me. I have often written that I had three dreams. Getting married had not been a dream that I had thought to put on the list. I now realize how important this reality is to me in my life.

I have been writing in this book about going beyond expectations. I think I went beyond anybody's expectations in getting married. People may look at an IQ and not want to look beyond to what could possibly be more. I am thankful that my wife Dee was able to look beyond my disability and see me as a husband and be willing to share life in our future together. I hope this helps you look beyond and not get locked into preconceived notions about persons with disabilities. Yes, of course I got married!

Chapter Nine
"Advocacy"

I want to share some thoughts about advocacy and how to be a good advocate on behalf of your own self. I feel that I have been a good advocate for myself for most of my life. I worked things out in my mind to get a clear picture of the situation. Then I envisioned the progression of steps to fulfill my plan.

I believe there are two principles involved in becoming a good advocate for your self or for a cause. First, you need to be in tune with how you feel. Secondly, you need to voice what you think about the issue in a clear and precise way.

In my own case I was a person who went beyond anybody else's expectations. I was born in early 1950's. I was born with cerebral palsy and was eighty-five percent cross-eyed. The authorities, at that time, were not particularly in tune to people with disabilities. Therefore, there were not a lot of services in every community as there are today. My mother and dad were advised by their doctor to seek out a special school for people with disabilities. The only school in North Dakota happened to be 250 miles away from my home. You can ask the question, was that a good decision for my parents to make and put me in a school that far away from home for eight years? My comment on that question is, "What other choice was there?"

The other part of this issue involved testing. They diagnosed me as having an IQ in the low 60's. Was the test biased against somebody that could not read and do things in the time allotted for the answer to be given? If so, the tests would show that the person had a low IQ. Based on that theory of timeliness, they recommended that the person (I am talking about myself) should be put into a special education program. So why did they make this decision? The decision was based on my disability and the fact that I could not talk. I had very few words in my vocabulary causing my verbal skills to be very low because of cerebral palsy. If the test did have a time limit on it I would not have had enough coordination to fulfill the time limit. Therefore, the test determined that I was to be put in special education for the rest of my formal schooling.

My argument in all of this is that as professionals they did not carefully understand my disability correctly.

The interesting thing about this misunderstanding, and the lack of education on their part, was that I wound up in the Crippled Children's school where I received regular education. But, when I left that school after the eighth grade, they recommended that I be put in special education rather than regular high school. Is it possible that they recognized that I had some speech problems and that they may have thought I had some learning problems as well? If I had been a professional at that time I would have re-tested the person to determine if that would be the right placement. But as far as I know, if they did any testing, the interpretation was wrong. Did they do this on purpose? We will never know.

I left the Crippled Children's school in 1965. I was enrolled in the fall of that year in special education class in the public school. We need to understand that special education was not available in public school until the 1960's when President John F. Kennedy was in office. So in 1965 special education was only two or three years old. It is my thought that they put me into special education because they did not know what to do with a person with cerebral palsy. Since I was diagnosed earlier with a low IQ, they took that diagnosis and placed me in the new special education class.

Today that would never have happened without tests confirming that I had some learning disability. I would imagine that one could say that was a period of time in our society when people were trying to understand people with disabilities and how best to give them an education. I imagine many of their discussions were not made with accurate understanding of some disabilities.

In my case I had, at that time, a clear mind and I knew exactly what I wanted to do with my life. The fact that I could eventually receive a university degree says something about what they were thinking about someone with cerebral palsy not being educable in regular classes. We can look back in history and see many mistakes that were made in false judgment and with inaccurate information. Hopefully we have evolved into new and effective methods and information in dealing with these issues.

As a person with a disability and as an advocate it is my goal to educate people about what happened in the past so it will not happen again. We need to learn from the past and recognize mistakes that have been made, but we cannot just focus on them. We need to go forward and continue to develop the ways and means to provide for tomorrow's children. This has been the case in many situations. Parents today have better resources at their disposal than my parents did.

I did not write this material to make people in my past feel guilty. I wrote it so that all of us could be thankful for the resources we have today and the new possibilities that will emerge to provide support and education for children with disability in their communities and with their families.

Community based programs are important. They give families choices that they never had before. It also gives persons options for their lives so they can live and interact in their own community. We have come a long way since the 1950's, but we still have a way to go.

Today we have people who still do not understand those who have disabilities. This lack of understanding is not only a problem for the individual with a disability and his or her family, but it is a problem for the whole society.

As we begin to talk about public education there is a need to continue to talk about the acceptance of persons with disabilities in the population of the public school. This has improved but there are still young people who experience a lack of acceptance and understanding by others.

The improvements that we have made, such as de-institutionalizing to allow people to live in their own communities, has helped this issue of acceptance. It has also helped financially for the families and communities. Many people have become more knowledgeable about different kinds of disabilities because they see these persons at community and neighborhood events. However, there needs to be continuing attention and education given to the issue.

In my work as a public advocate I have used certain questions to get at the experience of young people today. These are not scientific questions but probes into the way young people interact with each other with regard to disabilities of one kind or another. The question I ask most often is "How many of you have been teased because you might seem different?" In most groups of 50 to 75 people almost all of them raise their hands. The next question I ask is "How many of you have teased someone else because they look or act differently?" Surprisingly the same people raise their hands. I have asked this question all over the United States and the responses have been the same. If someone is different in our society, such as a person with a disability, they are apt to be teased or ridiculed.

I take a look at these unscientific results and I am puzzled. There may be several things at the bottom of this behavior. Some of it may come from the way they feel about themselves. Some of it may be related to fear. Or, it could be that they do not know how to relate to someone who appears different from him or her self. All of these reasons, and the others that I have not named, point to the importance of the work of advocacy. The key element in that teaching of advocacy is to help everyone understand that each person has at least one area in ones life that is not as "able" as others are. There are not just 53 million people in the U.S. that have disabilities. We are all in the same boat. We all have a chance to be who we want to be if we allow and assist each other to pursue each ones' dreams.

Chapter Ten
"Awareness"

The word "awareness" had become an important word for me. As I pondered that word I started to ask myself, "How do people perceive me as a person who has disabilities?" If I had written this chapter some years ago I would not have this language. This is a very interesting question for a person with visible disabilities. This question is one of the reasons why I started Break Through Inc. in 1978. I wanted to get at that specific question. Over the last thirty years I have discovered that there are many answers to that question.

My awareness that my disability brought on various perceptions began at an early age. When I was a kid I loved sports and wanted to be on a baseball team. Every time we chose up sides I was the last person taken. I knew that I was not the best baseball player on the field, but I wanted to be part of the team. The other kids saw me as a hindrance rather than an asset.

They were not able to look past my disability and see desire and the spirit I had to be a part of them.

There was a time, when I was much older, when I walked into a restaurant; I was greeted by the host who perceived me as being intoxicated. He saw my jerky movements and heard my slurred speech and jumped to a conclusion that I had been drinking. I did not have too much drink as it was morning and I only drink coffee in the morning. The host kindly asked me to leave the restaurant. Surprisingly, I took the initiative to begin talking to him about my disability.

Inside of twenty minutes he invited me to stay and have breakfast. I took the time to help this person understand who I really was and hopefully he was opened up to check his perceptions in the future. I am sure he remembered that conversation for a long time. He became aware of my disability. I hope he became more aware of his own disabilities that were probably hidden from view.

These examples explain why I had such a passion to start an organization like Break Through. It was born out of frustration of my own encounters with people who did not understand, nor were they very aware of the nature of various disabilities. Since 1978 Break Through has seen a lot of people come and go as volunteers and staff, but the basic mission and vision has not changed. Break Through is committed to educate people concerning disabilities. It hopes to bring people to an awareness to look beyond the disability of the person and see the assets this person brings to the situation.

I have been privileged to be part of hundreds of conversations about the whole issue of disabilities. These conversations always include bringing to light these persons with disabilities as persons and not what they should be like. I know first hand, as a person with cerebral palsy and a misdiagnosis of low intelligence, what it feels like to be treated as a second-class citizen. This is why I began Break Through Inc.

There were three of us who signed the corporation papers – Beckmen, Stedje and myself. We began an organization that in most part should not have lived so long. The resources were lacking. But, as the director I refused to let that stop me. Money was not the issue. A broadened awareness of the needs and affirmation of persons with disabilities was and that is why the organization was born.

Particular areas of focus for our work began to emerge. Break Through received a small grant of money in the early 1980's. We used this grant to explore the issues related to families of persons with disabilities. We wanted to understand the dynamics of facing disabilities as parents and siblings. This meant using the money to visit and interview families in various parts of the country.

I attended a conference on disabilities in Kansas City. One day I met a couple, Tom and Harriet Rose, who had a teen-age daughter with cerebral palsy. They were my first interviewees. The Rose's philosophy was that if there was a problem there had to be a solution. This was their approach to the whole situation of their daughter's disability. They realized there were many problems associated with this disability. They did not respond by focusing on the effects of the problem on them. They did not focus on the negative. They focused on the positive. They became strong supporters for their daughter and strong advocates for finding solutions of all kinds for the many problems they faced. I am thankful for the insight I gained through the Rose's approach to the issues. They modeled a positive and helpful approach. This was helpful to me. I was young and just beginning to learn from the perspective of the other side of the issues -- the side that is represented by the family of the person with a disability. I had much to learn about the way disabilities affect others who are caring for and supporting the person with the disability. Knowing and talking with the Rose's was a wonderful way to begin the research on working with families.

The day that I began the organization I realized that I had no experience or education in running a business. I just began putting this organization together as logically as I could. I knew that I had to have a board of directors, so I put one together. I had a secretary who handled correspondence and other duties in the office.

Rev. Beckmen helped me get in touch with youth around the country. I had many opportunities to speak with young people at youth gatherings, conventions and camps. Working with young people to bring more awareness and advocacy became a major focus of Break Through along with family support.

If money was the reason I began this organization, I would have been long gone. Awareness is the key as I have stated before. I wanted people to look at persons with disabilities as assets rather than hindrances. There are a lot of people with hidden disabilities or limitations. Most people only perceive physical limitations. I remember meeting a few people who seemed to have no disabilities themselves, but as I talked with them, as individuals, it became clear that they had a "hidden disability". Later they stated they did have learning problems.

We need to be sensitive to all individuals.

So What

Chapter Eleven
"IQ of 63- So What!-
What does it really mean?"

IQ of 63! Do they really mean that I was mildly retarded? I was diagnosed with an IQ in the low 60's. Yet, I graduated from the university with a grade point average of 3.29. Therefore I say "so what" to the diagnosis of 63.

I would encourage you to come to your own conclusions when dealing with other people that you also say --"So What".

When you look at some IQ charts (that can be found on the internet*), they indicate that IQ's between 60-74 states that a person could possibly attain a 6th to 8th grade education. Employment options would describe your ability as "slow, simple and supervised".

*http://www.geocities.com/rnseitz/Definition_of_IQ.html

Table 1 - Practical Significance of IQ

IQ Range	Frequency	Cumulative Frequency	Typical Educability	Employment Options
Below 30	>1%	>1% below 30	Illiterate	Unemployable. Institutionalized.
30 to 50	>1%?	>1% below 50	1st-Grade to 3rd-Grade	Simple, non-critical household chores.
50 to 60	~1%?	1.5% below 60	3rd-Grade to 6th-grade	Very simple tasks, close supervision.
60 to 74	3.5%?	5% below 74	6th-Grade to 8th-Grade	"Slow, simple, supervised."
74 to 89	20%	25% below 89	8th-Grade to 12th-Grade	Assembler, food service, nurse's aide
89 to 100	25%	50% below 100	8th-Grade to 1-2 years of College.	Clerk, teller, Walmart
100 to 111	50%	1 in 2 above 100	12th-Grade to College Degree	Police officer, machinist, sales
111 to 120	15%	1 in 4 above 111	College to Master's Level	Manager, teacher, accountant
120 to 125	5%	11 in 10above 120	College to Non-Technical Ph. D.'s.	Manager, professor, accountant
125 to 132	3%	1 in 20 above 125	Any Ph. D. at 3rd-Tier Schools	Attorney, editor, executive.
132 to	1%	1 in 50	No	Eminent professor,

137		above 132	limitations.	editor
137 to 150	0.9%	1 in 100 above 137	No limitations.	Leading math, physics professor
150 to 160	0.1%	1 in 1,100 above 150	No limitations	Lincoln, Copernicus, Jefferson
160 to 174	0.01%	1 in 11,000 above 160	No limitations	Descartes, Einstein, Spinoza
174 to 200	0.0099%	1 in 1,000,000 above 174	No limitations	Shakespeare, Goethe, Newton

When I got older I realized that my mental diagnosis of my IQ tests were always something that bugged the heck out of me. I never thought of myself as a person with a low IQ. I was always reminded, by others, of the things I could not do but I blew that thought away. I always wanted to be "average".

I was a typical boy that had dreams and thought to myself what I would do when I grew up. I shared earlier that I took long walks and thought about what I wanted to do with my life. I know that these tests of mine, as a young child, haunted my mother. She would often ask me and talk about how behind I was in comparison to other children. I realize my parents wanted to believe differently but couldn't shake the fact that I was tested by a professional and there was a battery of tests that I had taken. I was trying to understand how I could have a low IQ but I always thought I was intelligent. I said "so what" because I wanted to laugh it off. I wanted to make a joke of it and I am still able to make a joke of this. I have got to laugh at myself at the expense of other people's mistakes.

My IQ was based on the things that I knew when I was at the age of four. I had a very slight vocabulary and my hand/eye co-ordination was not the best so therefore those two drawbacks did not help.

The idea that I was tested with a Low IQ in the 60's was very apparent to me. It seems they did not take into consideration my physical disabilities. Also, the time restraints for taking the tests should not have been used because of those physical limitations. Today they probably would not look at the time limits to take the tests because they would want to separate the physical from the mental. One of the problems I had was that I could not put the 'relationships' of objects together at that early age. But of course my "mental age" and my "chronological age" eventually did catch up. That should be very apparent to what I have accomplished in my life.

I feel that the IQ tests given at a very early age without follow up tests or re-evaluation are not in the best interests of any individual. In my case, the drawbacks I had were less than a one hundred word vocabulary, my physical dexterity which was not "average" to begin with, because of the spasticity of my muscles and my lack of co-ordination. These were not in my best interests because they effected my mental evaluation in the IQ tests.

In the 1950's they probably did not know enough about people that were born with cerebral palsy (spastic quadriplegia) and it's neurological effects on me. This lack of information about cerebral palsy did not adequately prepare them to give any such "mental" IQ standards tests to a person with a physical disability. I was also born 85 percent cross-eyed. Based on the IQ criteria of the 1950's the professionals came up with an "average" for everybody.

In my case, because I did not receive re-evaluation until the year before I finished high school, I believe that my education was unnecessarily oppressed during those years. Eventually the education system did realize they made a mistake; as to my learning potentials. But that was too late to give me back those lost years. I should have been challenged with better education in my formative years in school. Special education classes, in those days, did not supply enough education to me and others that may have had more potential.

I was put into a category. I was put into a "box" so to speak. Let me tell you a story, a kind of a parable that I often use when I am giving presentations. I want to tell you this story to try to get my point across and I want you to think about how you re-act to it as you are reading it.

"One day there was a big box in this outside mall. People were gathered around this box during lunch to talk about what people talk about at lunchtime. The box was so big you could see it a block away. There were two children, about 3 to 5 years old, that saw this huge object and asked their mother if they could go over to it. Their mother was tired and wanted to go home as it had been a long morning shopping but gave up and replied, "Yes, we can do this." As they got closer they began to run towards this big box. They made their way through the crowd and up to the box. Of course the mother was in the back. The two children carefully examined the box. It was wrapped with nice gift wrap paper. The children wanted to unwrap the box. Suddenly, they heard a voice come from the box and it said, "Help me." Quickly the children began to unwrap and open up the box. They reached in and they grabbed the hand of this boy that had called from within the box and pulled him out. Seeing this, the crowd was amazed as they had seen this box in this mall before and never realized there was anything in it. The crowd began to ask questions. One of the very first questions was

"Why are you in this box?" The person replied by saying –"You put me in that box, by the way you treated me, by the way you looked at me, by the way you spoke to me and made fun of me. This box is a safe-haven for me and no body could attack me by their actions and words that they used to describe who I am, so I stayed in the box."

This person could very well be myself or any one else that has been treated wrongly by other people.

So do not let any preconceptions about abilities or disabilities cause you to re-act in a way that leads someone to find a hiding place in a box. Potentials are always there for everyone despite any one else's expectations. People bloom and grow with encouragement and being treated as "normal" because there really is no "normal" with any society. We all have abilities and must not put anyone in a "box".

So again I say "IQ of 63- So What!" Hopefully you will follow that train of thought as you go through life and interact with other people that may have different abilities.

Admittedly, the IQ tests today are being evaluated a little differently than when I was a boy. The chart below is stated on a current web page *. It reads:

"Mental deficiency used to be more finely classified using the following technical terms that later began to be abused by the rest of society.

IQ Range	Classification
70-80	Borderline deficiency
50-69	Moron
20-49	Imbecile
below 20	Idiot

These are now largely obsolete and mental deficiency is now generally called mental retardation. The following is the currently used classification of retardation in the USA (5)

IQ Range	Classification
50-69	Mild
35-49	Moderate
20-34	Severe
below 20	Profound

Moreover, "educable mentally retarded" is roughly equivalent to mild mental retardation, and "trainable" mentally retarded is roughly equivalent to moderate (5). The DSM now requires an assessment of a person's adaptive functioning as an additional criterion for labeling someone retarded. IQ is not enough."--unquote

Co-incidentally, and humorously, as I am writing this chapter on the computer, my "Weather Bug" icon on my computer desktop reads 63 degrees!!

So I am saying—"so what!" IQ's, like temperatures, apparently can change too!

*http://www.iqcomparisonsite.com/IQBasics.aspx

ADDENDUM -OPEN LETTERS

The underlying mission of Break Through is to help people be more aware of the needs of persons with disabilities. Awareness on our part is critical if the needs of those with disabilities are to be met at home, school and in the community. This chapter contains a series of open letters to various groups of people who interact with and support persons with disabilities. The phrase, "it takes a village to raise a child" could be translated to "it takes a coalition of parents, teachers, health professionals, businesses and other young people to affirm and support persons with disabilities, so that they may prosper and become all that they can become." I hope you will read these letters with an eye toward seeing the part you can play in increasing your own awareness and effecting the awareness of others in affirming and assisting persons with disabilities.

121

An Open Letter to Parents

It is my privilege to write and be honest to you as parents of a person with disabilities. I appreciate the hard work you do for your child. I know that you are trying to make a better life for him or her. I would like to share my experience as a person with disabilities with you. As a son, the biggest appreciation I had of my parents was that they loved me. Even though they probably did not know much about my disability when I was born, I had a deep sense of their love. Secondly, I want to say to you that you are the most important advocate that your child has, especially in working with health and educational systems. Your encouragement and advocacy on his or her behalf is the strongest voice that will have an impact on their lives.

Working with the school districts, that your child may attend, may be difficult, but I guarantee they also have the best interests for your child in mind. You can develop a good relationship with the school district and the teachers. What happened to me in my school was not my parent's fault. The professionals did not have the resources to understand my ability and give adequate guidance to my parents. Living in the 21st century, we find ourselves in a new situation. There are many more resources and much more knowledge available. Hopefully your community can provide these up-to-date resources. I hope you can discover the proper advocacy role to play in making your child's path open and productive to his or her life.

The voice of the parent is more important than anyone else's voice who may also love and respect your child. This is why I ask never to give up. It has been said that a good advocate is never satisfied because there is always more to do. There is always one fight to fight. There is one more person for whom to fight for.

Sometimes you might feel that you all alone in the struggle. I can guarantee that there are many loved ones that are in the same struggle. It is important to keep a sense of humor through it all. There will be days when you just need to stand back and laugh. Your work with your other children is very important as well. You may need to encourage them to understand and respect their sibling. They may need to serve as advocates as well, particularly in school and play situations. Hopefully, they will pick up the torch in their generation to serve as advocates for other persons with disabilities. This is one of the most important lessons you can share with all of your children.

Open Letter to Teachers and Professionals

As you read this book the thought that should have come to you is, how could this happen? How did I fall through the education cracks?

When I was in school Special Education was in its infancy. Because I was misdiagnosed with a low IQ, the teachers did not re-visit the diagnosis or re-test. I only say this to you so that you will be reminded to re-evaluate as you deal with people with disabilities whether as children or adults.

I have visited with many parents. One piece of advice they shared was for professionals to talk to them in language they can understand. Too many times you talk to them with language that makes them nervous. I realize that as professionals we have our own lingo but we need to understand that lay persons often do not understand the vocabulary and technical references we may use. Remembering that will also enhance the relationship of trust that needs to be built in this work.

I do not want to be all criticism and no praise. I realize that you, as professionals, work hard and try to make the best decisions. I want to be here as a reminder as we begin to communicate with people at a very sensitive time in their lives regarding their sons and daughters.

Thank you for your hard work and your willingness to help people to have lives that are fulfilling and productive. Your concern and your advocacy are important to thousands of people.

Open Letter to the General Public

One day I walked into that restaurant I referred to earlier and I had an opportunity to sit down and visit with the person who was about to ask me to leave. This was one of the most important conversations I had with a person on a one-to-one basis. He took the time to understand me as a person with a disability. My hope is that you will get to know someone who has a disability and experience them as a person just like yourself.

There are 54 million people with disabilities in the United States. They are in your community. They are in your schools and they are employees and employers. We all live together in community. It is important to remind ourselves that we all have shortcomings and disabilities. The next time you look at person with a disability understand him or her as you would want to be understood. Thank you for reading this important letter on awareness.

Open Letter to Businesses

One day I went to the city on business. I was meeting with a potential client. We had dinner and a great conversation about possibly working with his business and doing some awareness training with his employees. After our meeting I went to a hotel where I had made reservations. My bags had been dropped off earlier. I walked into the lobby of the hotel. The front desk was very busy. I stood in line until it was my turn to check in. At that time I did not have a state ID card. Because I did not have an ID card or a driver's license she asked me to leave. Now the question is, was it important for me to have an ID card or driver's license to check in or was that an excuse not to welcome me for the night? What do you do with this? How should one react to this? I know how I reacted but the important thing is how we, as a general public, react to this. I believe that that was discrimination. I believe she did not want me there and needed an excuse to tell me to leave. This event happened to me and it happens to a number of people every day. We need to be much more careful in how we perceive people in businesses that cater to the public. Many employees dealing with the general public are uncomfortable or totally lacking in awareness of many disabilities that can be confused with other problems. There are 54 million people with disabilities in this country, as I mentioned in one of the other letters. Every one of them has a right to be welcomed at a public or private business without being harassed and pre-judged by what they cannot do. Many people do need training for better awareness of the issues related to persons with disabilities.

An Open Letter to Students who will be Teachers

I have been where you are as I studied to get my degree in Vocational Rehabilitation. I write this specifically to my colleagues in college who will be teachers and leaders in our communities. I want to share my thoughts on being attentive, aware and responsible to the students, all of them, who will be your responsibility. I have struggled all of my life because a mistake was made concerning my condition as a human being by teachers and health professionals. I hope that you can refrain from prejudging your students. It is important for you to look at individuals as individuals, unique in many respects. Not all children can be lumped together.

I remind you that you need to be careful by not making decisions about your students based on records of those who have had them in class in previous years. Each student deserves a fresh start. Records concerning health and other information is important and needs to be recognized. But they are only information. They are data. They are not total predictors of the future of this student. Children grow over the summer. Children mature over the summer. There will be some new information to receive and explore in your relationship with this child. Children often far exceed someone's preconceived

129

expectations of that child. You have the potential to accept the child wherever that child may be in development and proceed to find ways to enhance and enable a greater potential for that child.

Do you remember a favorite teacher or coach in high school who helped you along in a special way? Wouldn't it be wonderful if a child came to you later and said that you had changed his or her life, or that you were the best teacher? It is very important that you stay open to the possibilities of every child who comes to you to learn. It is in your power to accomplish this.

Thank you for what you do for children.

1978-2008

Ben D. Anderson is the founder of Break Through Inc. which he began in 1978.

Break Through is a non-profit organization that provides leadership training to schools, universities, businesses, churches and parent and professional groups. The training enables them to build a new awareness of and sensitivity towards persons with disabilities. The message motivates people to face their discomfort and opens the door to better interpersonal relationships. Ben travels nationwide as the director and chief trainer of Break Through, Inc. He does keynote presentations and workshops.

For booking information please contact us at:

Email address: hy@bendanderson.com

Phone: (715) 554-1179

Please visit our website at:
www.bendanderson.com

131